DISCIPLINE

IS NOT A DIRTY WORD

Living from the Inside Out

ROBIN A. CIOFFI

DISCIPLINE IS NOT A DIRTY WORD
LIVING FROM THE INSIDE OUT

Copyright © 2020 by Robin A. Cioffi

Scriptures cited NASB are taken from the New American Standard Bible®, Copyright © 1960, 1962, 1963, 1968, 1971, 1972, 1973, 1975, 1977, 1995 by The Lockman Foundation. Used by permission.

Other scripture quotations cited—
AMPC: From the Amplified Bible, Classic Edition. © 1954, 1962, 1967, The Lockman Foundation. Used with permission.
ESV: From the Holy Bible, English Standard Version. New York: Oxford University Press, 2009. Used with permission.
KJV: From the Holy Bible, King James Version.
NKJV: From the Holy Bible, New King James Version. © 1982, Thomas Nelson, Inc. Used with permission.
NLT: From the New Living Translation, © 1996, 2007, Tyndale House Foundation. Used with permission.
NIV: Scriptures taken from the Holy Bible, New International Version®, NIV®. Copyright © 1973, 1978, 1984, 2011 by Biblica, Inc.™ Used by permission of Zondervan. All rights reserved.
TPT: The Passion Translation®. © 2017, 2018 by Passion & Fire Ministries, Inc. Used by permission. All rights reserved.
AMPC;

ISBN: 978-1-7351284-2-9

Published by:
OLIVE ORCHARD PRESS, LLC
CORAL SPRINGS, FLORIDA 33071
Printed in the United States of America

ACKNOWLEDGMENTS

I must first give thanks to my God for enabling me to write this book. I am forever grateful for your amazing grace and love beyond measure. I am Yours and You are mine...

Thank you to my precious parents and siblings for your constant love and care. I love you all so very dearly.

Thank you to Bishop Rick Thomas for encouraging me many years ago to write this book. I still remember your telling me that I had something to say and that people should hear from me.

Thank you to my beloved son, Daniel. You have reminded me to keep on dreaming and have encouraged me to continue fulfilling my God-given assignment. I love you more than words could ever express.

Thank you to Ellen Nestos for the countless hours you have sown into making this book a reality. I love and appreciate you so very much.

TABLE OF CONTENTS

INTRODUCTION

IT HAS BEEN SAID THAT ALMOST ALL FAILURE IS due to a broken focus. It seems reasonable then to say that with consistent and strong focus you will have success and victory. The question that begs to be asked is what are you focusing on? The Bible teaches and exhorts us to focus our thoughts upon the Word of God.

My purpose in writing this book is to encourage you and hopefully to even challenge you.

I am really amazed with the evidence that many of us are living defeated lives.

Rather than recognizing the power of Christ that's been deposited on the inside of our born-again spirit, we are being ruled by our own thoughts and emotions. Rather than choosing to be led by the Word of God, many of us are choosing to live life carnally-minded—just like the people around us—just like the world does.

If we are going to really learn to "walk by faith" we cannot live our lives being moved by our senses.

Remember, you are called to walk by faith and not walk by your feelings.

Today, more than ever, we must realize that "Christ in us is the hope of glory." We the church should be the most joyful and peaceful people in this world. I believe we are truly living in the last of the last days and we need to get back to the basics of choosing to live a spiritually disciplined life.

It really is a daily decision that you and I must make.

Are we going to be a people that choose to be led by the Spirit or are we going to be moved by what we see and feel? We must daily choose "to put on Christ." Choose you this day! I believe now is the time for the Church to begin looking like the Church. People are looking to us for the answers. You see we are to be different than the rest of the world. We have Christ and He is the answer to all of life's problems. He has given to us the very words of life.

However, too many times we who are the Church look no different than the rest of the world. Before we go any further, I'd like to offer you the best gift you will ever receive. If you're not yet a follower of Christ, today is your day. The most important truth you will ever hear is that God is a good God and He loves you. He really cares about you and wants you to get to know Him personally.

We read in John 3:16, *"For God so loved the world, that He gave His only begotten son, that whoever believes in Him shall not perish, but have eternal life."* (NLT) I want to invite you to pray a life changing but simple prayer.

The Bible says, *"If you confess with your mouth Jesus as Lord, believe in your heart that God raised Him from the dead, you will be saved; for with the heart a person believes, resulting in righteousness, and with the mouth he confesses, resulting in salvation"* (Romans 10:9,10 NASB).

If you would like to receive Jesus as your Lord and Savior, pray this simple prayer and mean it from your heart—

Jesus, I need You and I ask You to come into my heart today. I confess that I am a sinner and I am lost without You.

I believe that You died on the cross for me. I believe You shed Your blood that covers all my sin. Thank You for forgiving me and washing me clean. Thank You for making me whole.

Jesus, I believe that God raised you from the dead and that you are alive forevermore. I receive You now as my Lord and Savior. All that I am or ever hope to be, I give to You. All that You are, I now receive as mine.

I thank You, Lord, that today I am now a child of God, and I will never be the same.

In Jesus name. Amen

Precious one, if you just prayed that prayer, truly your life will never be the same. This will be the beginning of the most amazing journey of your life!

My prayer is that you will begin to discover that God has given us everything that we need to live victoriously in this life. Sadly, far too many of us are living depressed and discouraged lives. Beloved, this should not be so.

In this book, I will be sharing truths from God's word that have had a major impact upon my life. Not that I have arrived and always walk them out perfectly, but that is certainly my desire. These are some important keys that will enable you to walk in victory and overcome even through the trials of this life.

So what will you choose? My prayer is that you will choose today to begin "walking by faith and not by sight." The question is how do we do that?

Robin Cioffi

I
WHO ARE YOU?

THERE IS AN OLD SAYING, "WHAT YOU DON'T know won't hurt you." this couldn't be further from the truth. Honestly, the truth you don't know will really hurt and hinder you in every area of your life. It may also prevent you from fulfilling your God given purpose.

Today more than ever before, we see a society searching for identity. People are looking for purpose and for a sense of belonging. Unfortunately, the breakdown of the family is a major contributor to this dilemma. I believe this is also why so many young people fall prey to gangs and to the drug culture. They just want to find a place where they can be accepted and feel that they fit in.

Do you know your identity?
You see, the world is searching for their identity. They are really experiencing an identity crisis.

11

For the last five years, I have been ministering to women that have been incarcerated. I've had the privilege to lead many of these women to Christ.

What is surprising, though, is that many of these ladies had already received Christ before I personally gave them an invitation. Many had already confessed Christ before they ended up in jail. I used to ask myself, "How can this be possible? If they are really saved, then how have they ended up here?"

I can tell you why. They still don't know who they are. They are still identifying with the "old man."

They don't yet have the revelation of who they are now in Christ. They don't know or understand that certain rights and privileges belong to them as a child of God.

Sadly, this is the truth about many in the body of Christ. Yes, they are saved. Yes, they will go to heaven when they die, but they are not experiencing the abundant life of Christ that He has provided.

While going to heaven is certainly going to be beyond amazing, what about the here and now?

The church has done a good job of "getting people saved." but I'm convinced that we have not done so well in equipping believers to live victorious lives.

As believers in Christ, we must know our authority and what belongs to us. Jesus said, *"I have come that they may have life, and that they may have it more abundantly"* (John 10:10, NASB).

> **Jesus wants us to experience life to the overflow. Nothing missing, nothing lacking, and nothing broken.**

We must have a revelation of what God has already done for us. Unfortunately, many believers really have little concept of what Christ has provided for them through salvation.

Salvation comes with promises

Let's take a closer look at the word *salvation*. I would suggest that many Christians think that salvation refers only to their experience of receiving Christ, the forgiveness of their sins, and going to heaven when they die.

While this is indeed an integral part of salvation, it isn't the complete picture. Salvation is everything that Jesus purchased for us through the atonement. It all belongs to you now as a believer in Christ.

The Greek word *sozo* is translated as *saved* but means much more than just forgiveness. Salvation also includes our healing, our deliverance, our freedom and the abundant life. Salvation is everything that Jesus provided through his death, burial and his resurrection.

*Salvation is the whole package provided
for us by the price Jesus paid for us.*

It amazes me that many Christians don't really understand or comprehend just how much God loves them.

Maybe it's because many haven't experienced the love of an earthly father. Maybe they haven't ever really seen true love lived out before them.

Even if that is true, however, the love that God has for us is far beyond any human love imaginable. Even the very best parents will never be able to love you with the extreme love that God has for you.

We read in Ephesians 2:4, 5, *"God is so rich in mercy and He loved us so much; that even when we were dead because of our sins, He gave us life when He raised Christ from the dead. It is only by God's grace that you have been saved"* (NLT).

The good news of the gospel is that God loved the entire world so much that He sent Jesus to die in our place. We certainly didn't deserve it and we certainly couldn't earn it, but still He loves us.

God's love for us is so amazing, and we are the beneficiaries of this wonderful salvation.

I often think about the price God paid by sending Jesus to die for me. As a parent, I've even thought that if the situation were to ever call for it, I would be willing to die in my son Daniel's place—but, to die for the entire world? Now that's a different story. Yet that's what God did by sending Jesus to die in our place.

So why did He do it? Because you and I are that valuable to Him. He loves you and me that much.

This is the good news of the gospel: the "almost too good to be true" news.

God knew we would never be good enough and that we would not ever measure up to His standard of holiness, so He sent Jesus to die in our place.

God's Love Never Changes

Herein is our love made perfect, that we may
have boldness in the Day of Judgment;
because as He is, so are we in this world.
I John 4:17 KJV

This powerful scripture assures us that we can be confident in God's love for us. Sadly, many believers haven't yet really received His great love.

Yes, they can believe He died on the cross for the sins of the whole world. Yet for some reason they just do not seem to relate to God's love for them personally.

15

I believe religion has played a big part in this dilemma. If we are constantly looking at God's love as something we receive when we "do well," but lose when we mess up, we are really missing it.

God's love for you isn't schizophrenic. His love for you will never change no matter what you do or what you don't do.

**God knows everything about you and is
still madly in love with you.**

It's imperative that you really grasp this truth. You can't give away what you don't know you have. If you don't really believe you're loved by God, how will you be able to love others?

The truth is God loves you today more than any person ever can or ever will. His love never changes and His love will never fail. That is just so amazing. What a wonderful Savior!

We can rest assured that when God looks at us, He sees Jesus. He literally sees us "in Christ". Now that should give you real peace of mind and security.

Who Am I?

Ask yourself today, do I know who I am? If you have received Jesus as your Lord and Savior, you are no longer your own. You've been bought by the precious blood of Jesus. Jesus paid the ultimate price for us because we couldn't live overcoming lives without Him.

Are you still struggling with your past sins and failures? Ephesians 1:7 says, *"In Him we have redemption through his blood, the forgiveness of sins in accordance with the riches of God's grace"* (NIV).

Praise God! He doesn't see your sin or past any longer. It's all been covered by His blood and cast into the sea of His forgetfulness. He's forgiven you...and so you must forgive yourself.

I want to encourage you to stop focusing on yourself and your failures. Start focusing on His righteousness. Instead of being sin-conscious, we should be righteousness-conscious.

Don't ever forget that you are the righteousness of God in Christ Jesus. Take your eyes off of you and fix them on Jesus, the Author and the Finisher of your faith.

The Old You is Gone!

The only one interested in your past is Satan. He wants to use it to accuse and shame you. But the old you is gone!

One of my favorite scriptures is 2 Corinthians 5:17: *"If anyone is in Christ, he is a new creation. The old things have passed away and behold all things have become new"* (NKJV).

*If you're in Christ, you're not the same
person any longer. You are brand new.*

As a matter of fact, the old you is dead and the new you is alive in Christ. Your old sin nature isn't in control any longer and *"sin no longer has dominion over you"* (Romans 6:14 paraphrased).

If you have truly received Jesus Christ as your Lord, then your spirit has been born again. You have a new nature—*"for you have died and your new life is hidden with Christ in God."* (Colossians 3:3 NASB).

You are brand new on the inside. You are now God's child with His spirit living on the inside of you, and that is really something to be happy about!

Intimacy with God the Father

> *For you have not received a spirit of slavery
> leading to fear again, but you have received a
> spirit of adoption as sons by which we cry out
> Abba Father. The Spirit himself testifies with
> our spirit that we are children of God, and if
> children then heirs also, heirs of God and
> fellow heirs with Christ.*
> *Romans 8:15-17 NASB*

This beautiful passage of scripture promises us that we have been adopted by God Himself. We are His children because of His great love and concern for us.

Nobody loves us or tenderly cares for us like God does. We can cry out to Him as our *Abba*. *Abba* is an intimate name for father—closely coinciding with our English word, *Daddy*.

We have such intimacy with God that we can cry out to Him as our Daddy God who hears us when we call. Maybe you didn't know your earthly father, or maybe he wasn't a very good father to you. It may be that you have a wonderful earthly father. Whatever your situation, your Abba Father is the perfect Daddy and He calls you His own.

This is the powerful truth that I often minister to the ladies that ▓▓ are incarcerated. Many of them have had problems with drug abuse and that's often the reason they have landed in jail in the first place.

I believe that most of them have not seen or ever had a godly father in the home. That is why it is so important for them to realize how deeply loved they are by God.

Another problem that seems to be so prevalent is how they view themselves. Many of them would say they are addicts. That's how they identify themselves, and that really is so sad.

They still identify with the "old man"
instead of the truth.

The truth is, as believers in Jesus, they are no longer addicts. Jesus doesn't call them addicts—He calls them overcomers. Truly, their identity has changed, but now they need to begin seeing themselves differently. As believers in Christ, He's already provided their freedom.

New Identity

Let me ask you a question. How do you see yourself? If you're in Christ, then your identity has changed.

If you still see yourself as a sinner, you need to take a closer look. Jesus doesn't see you as a sinner anymore, and neither should you.

You are now a child of God saved by His amazing mercy and grace.

If you can really get hold of this truth, you won't continue struggling with your old way of life. Old habits and temptations won't stand a chance of messing with you any longer.

You must see the new you clearly. You must see who you now have become. You are now a new creation.

You are worthy because of Jesus and the sacrifice He made. He paid the ultimate price for you and has provided everything that you will ever need.

The founder of Abundant Life Church in Margate, FL, Papa Woody, as we so fondly called him, used to say, "The me I see is the me I'll be." This deceptively simple statement is actually very profound.

We are no longer to identify with our old life filled with sin and failures. We are to now identify with Christ and His spirit that lives on the inside of us.

If you have received Jesus Christ as Lord and have accepted for yourself this great salvation, then you are saved— *"you being born again not of corruptible seed but of incorruptible, by the word of God which liveth and abideth forever"* (I Peter 1:23 KJV).

The kingdom of God now resides on the inside of your born-again spirit.

2 Peter 1:3 assures us that *"His divine power has given to us everything that pertains to life and godliness, through the true knowledge of Him who called you by His own glory and excellence"* (NASB).

The truth is everything we need has been deposited in our born-again spirit. As He is so are we in this world.

This means that everything that belongs to Christ, now belongs to you through knowledge of Him.

Knowing God for yourself is the key.

He already knows everything there is to know about you. We, however, will spend the rest of our days getting to know Him more and more.

Spend time in His presence and in His word. The more you know Him the more you will love Him. The more you know Him, the more you will know just how deeply loved you really are.

The revelation of that truth is amazing and life-altering for us as believers. You and I have been fully equipped to live a victorious Christian life.

So ask yourself today, how do I see myself?

Are you still struggling with your old habits and hang-ups? If you answered yes to that question, then I want to ask you what nature are you identifying with? Or, what nature are you allowing to dominate you?

The truth is that Jesus has already provided His freedom so you can start walking in it.

In John 8:32, Jesus says, *"And you will know the truth, and the truth will make you free"*(NASB). Notice the scripture says, *"and you will know the truth."*

It isn't just the truth that you know about or just hear about. It's the truth that you believe and understand. You must take the truth and apply to your life.

We need a revelation of the truth of God's word. When we "know" a truth there will be no talking us out of it.

Do you struggle with your identity? Or maybe you don't like the face you see staring back at you when you look in the mirror? God has a different view of us—

You are a chosen generation, a royal priesthood, a holy nation, a people for God's own possession, so that you may proclaim the excellencies of Him who has called you out of darkness into His marvelous light; for you were once not a people, but now you are the people of God.
I Peter 2:9, 10 NASB

Chosen!

What does it mean to be chosen? It means you were hand selected or hand-picked by God. You are now royalty and a child of the King. If you have received Jesus as Lord, then you belong to Him. God has set you apart.

Not that we will always live our lives perfectly, but we are designed to fulfill His plan and purpose for our lives. May God help us to live our lives worthy of His calling.

Let me share another powerful scripture that will really minister to you. Ephesians 2:10 reads *"For we are His workmanship created in Christ Jesus for good works, which God prepared beforehand so that we would walk in them"* (NASB).

The word *workmanship* reads *masterpiece* in the New Living Translation. You're literally a work of art made by God. There is no one exactly like you in the earth. You are unique. You are God's handiwork. God made you for His purposes.

Verse 10 continues with the statement that God has prepared or prearranged good works for you to do. He did this long before we were born and it was by His perfect design.

God has a plan for your life that only you can fulfill.

Remember that truth the next time the devil comes with his lies. Or maybe it's the lies that you think about yourself or have even been telling yourself.

We are *"ambassadors for Christ, as though God were making his appeal through us"* (2 Corinthians 5:20 NASB).

God has called you and me to be His ambassadors. We are called to be His representatives to the world in which we live.

There is a truism that says, "You might be the only Jesus that some people will ever see." That really is the truth. You probably work with some of them every day. Some people may never enter the doors of a church building, but you are the "church" that they see and hear.

We are called to be salt and light in this world. We are His disciples and we're called to make disciples.

Let your light shine and look for ways to be a blessing to people. It may be something as simple as saying hello or giving someone a smile. Never underestimate the power and value of simple things. They very well may be life-altering for someone.

You can expect that God wants to use you and that you have the greatest purpose of all—to reach the lost and the brokenhearted, seeing them restored to relationship with their heavenly Father. What can be better than that!

You can rest assured with confidence that you are not a mistake. God made you by divine design. That is who you are!

God never called us to be human doings but human beings.

Just be who God has called you to be.

Now come into agreement with God's Word and you can start experiencing all that Jesus has planned for you!

2
WHAT'S WRONG WITH DISCIPLINE?

God has not given us a spirit of timidity, but of power and love and discipline.
2 Timothy 1:7

DISCIPLINE DOES NOT COME NATURALLY FOR us. As a matter of fact some of you are probably cringing at the very mention of the word. What is it about discipline that we dislike so much?

Why do we wrestle with living a disciplined life? It's not that we can't be disciplined but we do have to get to the place that we see the value in being disciplined.

The older I get the more I realize that discipline is not optional in my life. It really is an essential.

As Christ's disciples, we are called to follow Him. You can see the word *disciple* is contained in *discipline*. As disciples, we are not only to be pupils, but also imitators of our Teacher, Jesus. That's how you define a Christian. We are to be Christ-followers.

It truly takes discipline to become a disciple.

That's why I have a bit of a hard time when someone comes to Christ and they think they can continue to live the same old life without making any changes. We are to be continually changing and looking more like Jesus. We are on an exciting journey and we are in the process of transformation—a transformation that will never end.

What does it mean to be self-disciplined?

The definition of self-discipline means the ability to control one's feelings and to overcome one's weaknesses.

The word *discipline* comes from the Greek word *sophronismos* which literally means "saving the mind or a sound disciplined mind."

We read in 2 Timothy 1:7, "*God has not given us a spirit of fear but of power, love and a sound mind*" (NKJV). Did you notice that the scripture says a "*spirit of fear?*"

Let me assure you that if you're experiencing fear it's not from God. It is from the enemy of your soul.

The words "sound mind" are the same as "self-discipline." God has literally given us the ability to be self-disciplined. A sound mind is a disciplined mind!

We should ask ourselves this question. If He's already given it to us what's the problem? Could it be we've been looking for it to come from somewhere on the outside when the power to be self-disciplined has already been deposited on the inside of us?

Beloved you are deeply loved by God and He has given you the power to overcome in this life.

If you have received Christ, then the Spirit of Christ himself is living inside of your born-again spirit.

We are living in a time when having a disciplined life is critical. Every day we are surrounded by people who are fearful and disheartened. They know nothing about living or experiencing the abundant life found in Christ.

I need to make a decision and so do you. We must choose for our own selves whether we will begin to live spiritually disciplined lives. Sometimes, we are our own worst enemy.

It always comes back to us and our own choices. *"Choose you this day!"*

I've been around long enough to know that we human beings do what we really want to do. It doesn't really have anything to do with being too busy or not having enough time.

No, we choose to do what's really the most important to us. Life is truly all about our choices and decisions. We choose how we will begin each new day. We can't play the blame game and look at others. We must take responsibility for ourselves and for our own decisions.

In I Corinthians 9:24-27 we read—

> *Do you not know that those who run in a race all run, but only one receives the prize? Run in such a way that you may win. Everyone who competes in the games exercises self-control in all things. They then do it to receive a perishable wreath, but we an imperishable. Therefore I run in such a way, as not without aim; I box in such a way, as not beating the air; but I discipline my body and make it my slave, so that, after I have preached to others, I myself will not be disqualified. (NASB)*

Paul is speaking about how athletes compete to win the prize and the way they would accomplish this was choosing to discipline themselves. They learned to practice self-control.

In the same way, we have to train ourselves to think right by focusing on God's Word. Just as a runner in the Greek games would run to win, so we Christians are in a race that we are called to win. Discipline and self-control are necessary for athletes, and they are just as necessary for believers.

The Fruit of the Spirit

> *The fruit of the Spirit is love, joy, peace, longsuffering, kindness, goodness, faithfulness, gentleness, **self-control.** Against such there is no law. And those who are Christ's have crucified the flesh with its passions and desires.*
>
> *Galatians 5:22-24*

Notice that the fruit of the Spirit includes self-control. This literally means you have the ability to be self-controlled because the Spirit of God is inside you. The fruit of the Spirit is deposited on the inside of your born -again spirit.

If we are going to bear spiritual fruit, we must discipline our thoughts, attitudes and our emotions. You see we have the fruit of self-control and it is discipline.

When the fruit of the Spirit of self-control is manifested in our lives as believers, we will be able to resist temptation and persevere through the trials of life.

Most of us will never become professional athletes but we will become powerful, overcoming Christians if we have self-control in all things.

Every area of our life is affected by self-control. Whether we choose to exercise self-control or choose to ignore it is up to us.

> Whoever heeds discipline shows the way to
> life.
> Proverbs 10:17 NIV

As believers in Christ, we are all in the process of change, or you might say we are all on a lifelong journey.

Maybe the Holy Spirit has been speaking to you about changes that you need to make. Change will always involve a choice and a decision that we need to make.

Whatever you allow and tolerate in your life will not exit your life.

What are you tolerating? Distractions, wrong relationships, a new job—or something else that the Holy Spirit has been showing you.

Remember that what you're willing to change in your life will determine how you walk into the future that God has for you.

We all know that change can be hard. Without real desire to change and a made-up mind to change you probably won't!

Our choices and discipline are interrelated. You won't make any real progress without both working together.

What is so wonderful is that you're not in this alone. The Holy Spirit, the Helper, is always there to lead, enable and empower you. Every new day brings opportunities for us to make choices and decisions.

The definition of the word "choice" is the act of selecting or making a decision when faced with two or more possibilities.

Throughout our lifetime we will make decisions that will either impact our lives positively or negatively. Everything we do in life involves a seed. We must learn to sow good seeds into our lives. The most valuable seed we can sow is the Word of God.

The Word provides the answer

I would like to share with you some scriptures that have greatly impacted my life in the area of making good choices and necessary "course corrections."

Be anxious for nothing, but in everything with
prayer and supplication with thanksgiving let
your requests be made known to God.
Philippians 4:6 NKJV

The apostle Paul is giving us the formula to living life without being overwhelmed by anxiety. Anxiety-causing situations will still come against you, but you can *"choose"* to not be anxious.

So many people today battle with anxiety. May I suggest that if you're one of those people, you can choose to do something about it. You just need to shift your focus.

What are you thinking about? What are you dwelling on? Do you have stinking thinking?

If you do, please take heart because there is something you can do about it.

You have been given the ability to choose what you will allow yourself to think about. You can choose to set your mind and thoughts upon the Lord.

Isaiah 26:3 says, *"You will keep him in perfect peace whose mind is stayed on Him"* (NKJV). This isn't always easy to do, but it is possible. Sometimes, this means choosing moment by moment to keep your thoughts centered upon the Lord.

It takes discipline, determination and a made- up mind.

The older I get the more determined I get. I am not going to allow anything or nothing to steal my peace.

The word "peace" in Hebrew is *shalom. Shalom* is God's peace. It's undisturbed, perfect peace—the nothing broken and nothing missing kind of peace. We experience that kind of peace when we keep our thoughts fixed on God and His word.

That kind of peace can't be shaken because we are trusting in Him. No matter the circumstances that may be surrounding us, we remain confident that God is always true to His word. He is *always* good, *always* true and *forever* faithful.

Another one of my favorite passages is found in Colossians 3:1-3—

Therefore if you have been raised up with Christ, keep seeking those things that are above, where Christ is, seated at the right hand of God. Set your mind on things above and not on the things that are on the earth, for you have died and your life is hidden with Christ in God. (NASB)

35

We must daily choose to seek after the Lord. We can choose to set our minds on things above or let the things here below capture our thoughts. It's our choice!

There's really nothing better than experiencing God's peace and joy. I choose to take hold of them for myself. I hope you will too.

You can't change someone else

We all know that making changes in our personal lives can be challenging to say the least. But when it comes to trying to change other people…well, you might as well forgot about it.

I need to be honest and admit that for many years I tried to change people. I have since learned that I can't change anyone and no one can make me change. Decision-making is our own choice.

Yes, we can encourage others to change but true change only happens when we individually and independently make the decision to change. We must make up our own minds if we're going to change—or not.

Our lives are made up of a series of decisions. The more we choose to be led by our flesh or our carnal nature, the more "in charge" our flesh becomes. On the other hand, the more we choose to be led by the Spirit, the flesh loses its strong hold.

We must choose to follow the leadership of the Spirit.

Lack of discipline is so rampant in our culture today. We must choose to discipline ourselves if we are going to walk in obedience and victory.

God has called us to walk by faith, but how are we going to do that if we choose to allow ourselves to live in the realm of our senses, moved by what we see, hear and feel.

There is nothing more powerful than living a Spirit-led life. However, the only way we can do this is by knowing the Word and then choosing to live by the Word of God.

Hosea 4:6 says, *"My people are destroyed for a lack of knowledge"* (KJV).

God has promised in His Word that *"He will not withhold any good thing from us."*

We won't fail if we know what God has given to us. His great and precious promises belong to us so we must take ownership of them.

Our responsibility is to feed on His Word and to follow the leadership of the Spirit of God that lives inside of you.

3
CHANGE YOUR MIND AND YOU'LL CHANGE YOUR LIFE

Do not be conformed to this world (this age), [fashioned after and adapted to its external, superficial customs], but be transformed (changed) by the [entire] renewal of your mind [by its new ideals and its new attitude], so that you may prove [for yourselves] what is the good and acceptable and perfect will of God, even the thing which is good and acceptable and perfect [in His sight for you].
Romans 12:2 AMPC

IT'S BEEN SAID THAT IF YOU CAN CHANGE your mind you can change your life. This is the truth. So how do we change our minds? It is quite simple. You can choose to apply the Word of God to your thought life. It really is all about our focus.

As we learn to focus on God's word and not our feelings, we will experience His peace. Not only that, but we will continue to grow and become spiritually mature. I truly believe that most of our problems would be solved if we would just practice renewing our minds and begin thinking right.

We are to think like God thinks.

We read in John 6:63, *"It is the Spirit who gives life, the flesh profits nothing; the words that I have spoken to you are spirit and are life"* (NASB). What does it mean to be carnal or fleshly? I used to think that being carnal meant being sinful. I've discovered that isn't always the case.

To be carnal means that you are led or dominated by your five senses. You are living your life in the natural. We must get our souls into agreement with the Word of God if we are going to live Spirit-led lives.

I'm not just referring to a head knowledge about the Word, but truly understanding and comprehending it for yourself. We need to daily spend time in the Word and allow it to speak to us. Only then will we begin to apply the Word to our lives and then experience being led by the Spirit.

Walking in the Spirit is having your soul in agreement with the Word of God. Remember your soul is your mind, will and emotions. The truth is that while God is not a respecter of persons, He is a respecter of principles.

As we choose to be led by the Spirit instead of our carnal nature, change will begin to happen. As we think the right thoughts we will make the right choices. This in turn will cause us to take the right actions and thus will bring about the right results.

> *Truly right thinking leads to right believing which will then lead to right living.*

It is so common to hear people say I believe in God, or maybe you share a truth from God's word with someone and they say, "Oh I believe that." Yet their life appears to be very different from what they say they believe. You see if you really believe something you will act in agreement with it.

I'm convinced that many people say they believe but yet they don't really have a revelation of the truth. Their belief is simply a head knowledge.

What does it mean to believe?

The definition of the word "believe" means to accept something as true. Nelson's Bible Dictionary says "belief" is to place one's trust in God's truth. A person who believes is the one who takes God at His word and trusts in Him for salvation.

One definition of faith is the "confident belief in the trustworthiness of a person, idea or thing. Belief that doesn't rest on logical proof or material evidence." Our belief and faith in God's Word will move us beyond the natural circumstances and beyond our natural senses.

Truly right believing changes everything.

You may say that sounds really good but I'm walking through some very hard things right now. The truth is we all have challenges in this life. No one is exempt from trouble. The important thing to remember is that you will walk through them. This too shall pass.

The real question is "how" will you walk through them?

We know the enemy always wants us to focus on what we don't have instead of what we do have. He wants us to keep our focus on the problems instead of focusing on our God who has all the answers- to those problems. The good news is that we can change our focus.

Romans 12:2 tells us, *"Do not be conformed to this world, but be transformed by the renewing of your mind, so that you may prove what the will of God is, that which is good, and acceptable and perfect"* (NASB).

This literally means don't allow the world to squeeze you into their mold and their way of thinking.

Go turn on your television and in about ten seconds you can see how messed up the world is with their thinking. But I have really good news for you. God's word has transforming power to radically change us from the inside out. His word is alive. We, however, must choose to take hold of it for ourselves.

What does it mean to be transformed?

It literally means a *metamorphosis*. That is, to change the form or nature into something completely new or different.

Look at the life of the butterfly. The butterfly doesn't start out as a beautiful creature. It is just an ugly caterpillar. As the caterpillar goes through the process of change it becomes that gorgeous butterfly.

The Greek word "*metanoia*" means repentance, a change of mind, conversion. Literally it means a decision to turn around and face in a new direction.

The living Word of God renews and changes our thinking. It will actually give you a total makeover, causing you to radically change into another person.

So ask yourself: Do I want to be transformed?

Transformation doesn't happen overnight, but the responsibility rests upon us to feed, respond and to move out on His word.

I have been walking with the Lord for forty years now. I still choose every day to feed my mind and heart on the Word of God.

I can't live a victorious Christian life without the Word and neither can you, dear one. The Word is our daily bread and we can't make it without it.

Let's look again at the rest of verse 2 of Romans 12: *"That you may prove what is that good, and acceptable, and perfect will of God."* The word *"prove"* literally means to make manifest to your natural senses. In other words, as we renew our minds by feeding on God's word, it will be made clear or evident to us what His will is for our lives. That is so powerful.

The Word of God will so transform our thinking that we can in turn carry out His plan for our lives.

I was reading a powerful story the other day found in I Samuel 13. This story takes place with King Saul waiting in Gilgal for Samuel the prophet to return to offer up the burnt offering. Saul has been waiting and the seven days had passed that Samuel had set for his return. Saul became very impatient and fearful while he waited for Samuel's return. Saul then made the decision to take matters into his own hands. He chose to offer up the burnt offering himself which was not his lawful or rightful duty.

44

He no sooner finished the deed when the prophet Samuel returned. Now here is the part I really want you to get in your spirit—

Saul began immediately to offer excuses and said, *"I thought, now the Philistines will come down against me at Gilgal, and I have not sought Lord's favor. So I felt compelled to offer the burnt offering myself"* (I Sam 13:12 NIV).

This was Saul's fatal mistake. He didn't choose to discipline his mind and emotions. He allowed fear and his own impatience to rule him. This in turn caused him to make a very bad decision which was then followed by a very wrong action.

The result was devastating. Saul lost his kingdom rule forever.

We can all learn a valuable lesson from Saul's tragic story. We will always get ourselves into trouble and off the path God has for us when we begin leaning to our own thoughts and understanding. We cannot give place to fear and anxieties that would cause us to act foolishly and impatiently. We must first and foremost keep the Word of God in our minds and allow it to rule our thinking.

Change Isn't Always Easy

Change isn't easy and you'll discover change doesn't always feel good. Ask anyone who has tried to break an old habit. First, you must have the desire to change. God will even give you the desire to change if you'll just ask Him. Change can be hard when it comes to breaking our old way of thinking and our old mindsets. God isn't going to defend your mind for you; it's your responsibility. You must make a decision for yourself.

Begin by defending and guarding your mind. So how do you defend your mind? You do so by capturing the wrong thoughts when they come into your mind.

We all have wrong thoughts that can come against our mind. Satan's desire is to get you to receive the negative thoughts and then act on them. However, you can choose to cast down wrong thoughts by replacing them with God's Word. The truth is, God is the one who has given us the authority to resist the devil and his lies.

We must choose to have a mindset that agrees with the Word of God. The Word of God is our only defense against wrong thinking. Wrong thinking leads to wrong living. Right thinking and right believing will lead to right living. A carnal or fleshly mindset profits nothing, but when I declare the truth of God's Word, the carnal mindset is defeated.

Before we ever speak a word, we have first had a thought.

Our thoughts are so powerful. They can bring life or they can bring death. You can choose to guard your mind and choose the thoughts you will allow to come inside. You can do it, beloved!

We need to allow the Word of God to speak to us in our inner man. We can choose to feed our minds the Word and it will change the way we think and what we see.

I want the Word to rule and reign in my heart so that I'm moved by the Word only. That's real maturity. I haven't arrived there yet, but I am on my way. I 'm further along in this journey of faith today than I was yesterday.

We should feed on the Word of God every day and our minds will be transformed. Remember this Christian life is a journey.

We read an interesting verse in the story of the Prodigal Son in Luke 15. Verse17 says, *"but when he came to himself"* (NKJV), he decided to go home to his father. He literally came into his right mind. He had a change of mind that changed the course of his life. That is so powerful!

How can we be led by the Word of God? We have to change our mindset by changing how we think. The carnal mind is the mind of the flesh. Our natural mind is programmed to think in line with the natural man. It's our flesh.

The carnal mind is dominated by our five senses. If we think in line with the world, we will have wrong thinking. The Bible says "*to be carnally minded is death.*"

So how can we begin to think right?
Only through the Word of God.

We must learn to get our souls into agreement with the word of God. If we don't learn to control our thoughts, we won't be able to control our emotions and, in turn, our actions.

I have an amazing testimony. I received Jesus Christ as my Lord and Savior in February of 1980. I was gloriously saved and delivered from a lifestyle of drugs and alcohol abuse. I can honestly say I was truly delivered, and the desire for my old way of life was taken away from me. I became a new creature in Christ Jesus.

However, I had decisions to make and steps to take every day so I could continue to walk in my newly found freedom. Through the help of the Holy Spirit, I made the decision that I would begin reading the Word of God every morning.

I purposed to set time aside every day to focus upon the Lord—time set aside to just be alone with Him and to really get to know Him personally for myself.

Notice I said through the help of the Spirit I made this decision. It's important to remember that we must make the decision. The Holy Spirit is a gentleman and He won't make you do anything. You get to decide for yourself, but we can rest in knowing that the Holy Spirit is right there with you, enabling you.

The Basics

I chose to apply what I like to call the "basics" of spiritual discipline: Reading the Word of God, praise and worship, prayer, attending church services, sowing my tithe and offerings, and fellowshipping with other believers.

We really do need to practice all of the basics to become rooted and grounded followers of Christ.

I have experienced such radical transformation and it has come from sowing the Word of God into my life. You see it isn't just the truth that sets you free. It's the truth you know that sets you free. The Word of God will do that for you too.

Everything in life involves a seed of some kind. We can allow good seeds or bad seeds to be sown into our lives. God's Word is the best seed we can ever sow. There isn't a single problem or situation that the Word of God doesn't solve.

Our behavior won't change unless we first change our minds.

You might make some changes through self-effort but they will only be temporary. True and lasting change comes about through a changed mind.

We need to be diligent about sowing the seeds of His Word and allowing them to change our thinking. Remember that right thinking leads to right believing. Allow the seed of His word to change your thinking, and then your thoughts will line up with the truth. If your thinking is right, then you will live right.

The Word has the power to change the way you think and it will radically change you into a different person.

A life-long process.

Today we live in what I like to call the "microwave society." Think about the last time you drove up to a drive through to place an order for some food or a cup of coffee. What happened if you had to wait even for three minutes? Maybe you became just a little impatient. Why is that?

Honestly, I think we have all been guilty of this. We want what we want and when we want it. We want it *now!*

The challenge is that our Christian walk doesn't happen at the snap of our fingers. Our Christian life is a journey—a journey that will last for our entire lives.

Renewing our minds is just like that. It's a lifelong process. We must reprogram our minds and our thinking by the Word of God. We are to be continually changing from our old way of thinking.

Now that we are in Christ, we have a new identity and must learn to identify with our new nature. We are going from strength to strength and glory to glory. We can think like God thinks.

We can think His thoughts because scripture says, *"We have the mind of Christ."* This isn't referring to our natural mind however.

The mind of Christ is in our born-again spirit.

That is why it is essential that we renew these natural minds with God's Word to bring about change.

We must take the time to allow God's Word to paint on the canvas of our hearts. That is the only way that we can have His mindset and see life His way. We need to change so we can help empower others to change.

I have found Philippians 4:8, 9 to be a wonderful passage of scripture for keeping my thoughts disciplined—

For the rest brethren, whatever is true, whatever is worthy of reverence and is honorable and seemly, whatever is just, whatever is pure, whatever is lovely and lovable, whatever is kind and gracious, if there is any virtue and excellence, if there is anything worthy of praise, think on and weigh and take account of these and fix your minds on them.

Practice what you have learned and received and heard and seen in me, model your way of living on it, and the God of peace, of untroubled, undisturbed well-being will be with you. (AMPC)

I have recently started reading the Passion Translation of the Bible, and I really enjoy it. It's nice to change things up a bit from time to time.

Look at this scripture in the in the Passion Translation—

So keep your thoughts continually fixed on all that is authentic and real, honorable and

admirable, beautiful and respectful, pure and holy, merciful and kind. And fasten your thoughts on every glorious work of God praising Him always.
Philippians 4:8, 9

Don't you just love how that reads so beautifully? The truth here is that you choose to keep your thoughts and focus on Him, on His promises.

Overcoming Adversity

The apostle Paul wrote the book of Philippians. If anyone could have had negative thoughts and circumstances to deal with, it surely would have been Paul. He was thrown in jail numerous times, beaten and shipwrecked, just to name a few of the many challenges that he had to face.

So what did he do? Did he just fall apart just like a cheap suitcase? Did he sink into depression? Did he just throw in the towel and say, "I'm just going to give up?"

We know from scripture that he didn't deal with his struggles and trials that way at all. Paul chose to put his thoughts on the Lord, and he kept his thoughts fixed on the Lord. He also reminded himself of the goodness of the Lord.

We can all certainly learn a valuable lesson here from Paul. We, too, need to remind ourselves of the goodness of the Lord.

Has He ever been good to you? Has He ever come through for you before? I know you're saying, "Of course He has!"

I want to encourage you today to remind yourself of His faithfulness. Call to remembrance all of your many blessings. You see it really is supernatural what happens to us when we choose to focus on the Lord rather than our problems. We can't stay down or depressed when we fix our thoughts on Him!

Isaiah 26:3 says, *"You will keep him in perfect peace whose mind is stayed on you, because he trusts in you"* (ESV). We can learn to fix our minds and thoughts upon the truth. We must choose, however, to be focused and intentional about it.

No one else is in charge of how we think. It's our responsibility, and we can learn to think right by lining up our thoughts with the Word of God. We can learn to keep our thoughts continually fixed upon Him.

Do you know someone who has battled with depression or discouragement? Maybe that's the place you find yourself right now. Did you know that you don't have to be depressed or discouraged?

Depression is really about us being "inward" focused instead of being "upward" focused or God-focused.

Depression and discouragement come about by focusing on the issues or challenges instead of focusing on the Lord. That is just how the enemy operates. He wants you to focus on the issues in your life instead of focusing on God's promises.

The truth is, if you're experiencing these feelings, you may simply have a "thinking" problem.

The enemy tries to bring those negative feelings and thoughts to us all. No one is exempt from his attempts.

Our life will go in the direction of our most dominant thoughts. You can either let your thoughts push you around, or you can push your thoughts around.

You get to choose what to do with those thoughts when they come against your mind.

You can choose to change your thinking. Go to the word of God and allow it to replace the bad thoughts. Beloved you really don't have to have another depressed day. It's really your choice.

Cast Your Cares

We read in I Peter 5:7, *"Casting all your anxiety upon Him because He cares for you"* (NASB).

That is the truth. God really does care about everything you care about. Your shoulders were just never meant to carry any of those cares. You can cast them upon the Lord. Place them at the foot of the cross and leave them there. He's well able to take them and carry them for you.

Right now if what you are thinking about, pondering and meditating upon isn't bringing you peace and undisturbed well-being, you're just wasting precious time thinking about the wrong things! Turn your thoughts towards Jesus and feed upon His goodness and His faithfulness.

I believe I can safely say that most, if not all, of our problems could be solved by simply learning to take God at His word—not just a head knowledge, but really believing, understanding and comprehending the truth that we're reading.

I'm sure we can all agree that reading the Bible is a very good thing for us to do. However, just reading like you're reading a good book isn't going to be enough.

We actually need to read and then meditate on what we've read.

His delight is in the law of the Lord and in His law he meditates day and night. He will be like a tree firmly planted by streams of water, which yields its fruit in season and its leaf does not wither; and whatever he does, he prospers".

Psalms 1:2, 3 NASB

Joshua 1:8 states, *"This book of the law shall not depart from your mouth but you shall meditate on it day and night so that you may be careful to do according to all that is written in it; then you will make your way prosperous and then you will have success" (NASB).*

Meditate in the Word

Some people are frightened by the word *"meditate."* Unfortunately, when we hear the word *"meditation,"* we automatically think of new age or other false religions.

Meditation was God's idea from the very beginning.

To meditate means to ponder, to rehearse, to think about, to remind yourself, to speak the word out loud to yourself and to roll it over in your mind.

Literally it is the picture of a cow grazing in the pasture. They eat and chew and swallow. The digestion process continues with the cow resting for a while. She then brings the food back up and begins chewing "the cud." The average cow spends over 6 hours a day eating and drinking.

While I know this is not a very pretty picture, it does bring clarity to how we are to meditate on God's Word. I have found that one of the best ways to meditate is to continue reading until you come to that one verse that really speaks to you. Sometimes it's like the word literally "jumps" right off the page at you. We need to take time to study God's Word.

Take each scripture and read it slowly and out loud to bring more clarity and understanding. Take that one verse and memorize it, think about it, ponder it and reflect upon it, and then you *"will make your way prosperous and then you will have success"* (Joshua 1:8).

As a young believer, I used to read many chapters of scripture every day. I have to admit that many times I was just performing a religious activity. It was on my daily list of "things to do." I read my Bible today so I could check that off my list.

While reading chapters of the Word of God is never wrong or a bad thing, how much are we really understanding? What truth have you gained from your time spent in the Word? You see it really isn't about how much time you are spending reading, but rather how much are you receiving?

*The Word of God contains the very
words of life that we need to live a
victorious life. It's the truth we know
that sets us free.*

I want to encourage you to try this simple exercise. Begin by reading three or four verses of scripture. Slowly read them out loud to yourself. Take each word and allow the Holy Spirit to speak to you. Meditate on the words you're reading. Allow His Word to paint a picture on the inside of you.

Here is an example to help you get started. Read Psalms 1:2, 3, again, aloud: *"But his delight is in the law (Word) of the Lord, and in His law he meditates day and night. He will be like a tree firmly planted by streams of water which yields its fruit in its season; and its leaf does not wither and in whatever he does, he prospers."*

Doesn't this passage paint such a beautiful word picture?

God Meant for His Word to be Personal!

We are to take the scriptures personally and apply them to ourselves. I even like to put my name in the verse as I read and study. I say, *"Robin delights in the word of the Lord, Robin meditates day and night. Robin is like a tree firmly planted."* That means I'm strong, stable and resilient. Go ahead and put your name in the verses and see yourself that way, too. We are fruitful and we are prosperous. Are you getting the idea? We just need to slow down and "feed" on His word.

Have you been asking God to speak to you? I want to tell you something, beloved—

Every time you make the decision to
feed upon His word, He speaks to you.

We will need to continue the lifelong journey of renewing our minds with the Word of God until Jesus comes. Why? So that our heart and mind will be in agreement. You could also say until you become "one with the Word."

The more we meditate on the Word of God, the more we will truly know Him. Jesus is the Word, He is the Word made flesh.

If we are not in the Word, renewing and changing our mindset, we will not be able to walk and be led by the Spirit.

Who We Are in Christ

Walking in the Spirit is knowing who we are in Christ. Who we are in Christ is more important and more real than what we can see or feel in the natural.

Walking in the Spirit means that you first see what you believe, rather than believing what you see. We want to become so mature in Christ that we are not moved by what we see or feel in the natural.

We will only be moved by what the Word of God says. What an exciting way for you and I to live! We're not alone on this road to change and transformation. We have the Spirit of God and His Word right there to help us all along the way.

Diligent and Intentional

We must be diligent and intentional. Make the decision to put forth the effort to renew your mind with the Word of God.

As we daily read, meditate and study the Word we will be able to speak and confess the Word with authority. We won't give up or let up until we have our manifestation of His promises.

Remember, God's plan for your life is always good and His Word is true. Begin thinking His thoughts and you will become the victorious child of God that He's called you to be!

4
GUARD YOUR HEART

Keep and guard your heart with all vigilance
and above all that you guard, for out of it flow
the springs of life.
Proverbs 4:23 AMPC

INSIDE YOUR BORN-AGAIN SPIRIT YOU HAVE the *"mind of Christ"* (I Corinthians 2:16), and it is always believing correctly. Our souls, however, must be trained to come into agreement with our spirits.

When we talk about the soul, we are referring to our mind, our will and our emotions.

I am thankful that the Lord has given us our emotions. This is an area of our lives that requires much attention and effort to keep under control. The answer is that we must learn to keep our hearts centered upon the Lord.

I want to share one of my favorite passages of scripture with you.

Proverbs 4:20, 21 reads—

My son, give attention to my words, incline your ear to my sayings. Do not let them depart from your sight; keep them in the midst of your heart. (NASB)

Or you could say it this way: Keep His Word abiding in your heart and thoughts.

The Hebrew word *levav* is the word used here for heart, and the meaning encompasses our thoughts, our will, our discernment and our affections.

Our heart condition truly affects every area of who we are.

So where do we begin? First, we begin by being intentional to feed ourselves the Word of God. We give it our attention and then we choose to submit to it.

This literally means that we are to keep our focus centered on God's Word as well as keeping it abiding in our hearts. We are to fill our thoughts with God's Word.

Proverbs 4:22 goes on to tell us that God's word is *"life to those who find it and health to all their body"* (NASB). God's word is our medicine. It brings healing to every part of our being—physically, mentally and emotionally.

Proverbs 4:23 says, *"Above everything else guard your heart, because from it flow the springs of life"* (ISV) The Amplified Classic Version reads, "*Keep and guard your heart with all vigilance."* Vigilance means the action or state of keeping careful watch for possible danger or difficulties.

Another translation reads, *"Keep your heart with all diligence."* Are you getting the picture? It takes persistent work and effort on our part. We can't have a nonchalant attitude towards guarding and protecting our heart. We must take this scripture truth seriously.

In the Hebrew, *"shamar"* is the word for *"keep"* and is also interchangeable with the word *"guard"*. It means *"to set a watch or a watchman over it."* It can also mean to *"put a hedge about."* How do we do that for our hearts?

I believe we can do that best by submitting our feelings, emotions, thoughts and desires to the Word of God.

I've heard Joyce Meyer say, "You can be pitiful or you can be powerful, but you can't be both."

We are powerful when we allow the Word of God to dominate our thoughts.

Any time we have a thought or feeling that is contrary to the Word of God we are faced with a decision. We can either let those thoughts and feelings run wild or be can bring them captive to the obedience of Christ. (See 2 Corinthians 10:5.)

Let's continue to read Proverbs 4:25: *"Let your eyes look directly ahead and let your gaze be fixed straight in front of you"* (NASB).

The Passion Translation makes it even clearer: *"Looking straight ahead with fixed purpose; ignore life's distractions."* This shows us that you can change the direction of your life by changing the direction of your heart.

I'm reminded of the story found in Luke 10. Jesus has come to visit the home of Mary and Martha. Jesus is seated quickly and He begins sharing truth with the other guests.

The scripture tells us that Mary immediately sat down at His feet, but Martha was busy making preparations for her guests. The scripture says, "She was distracted." Martha becomes so frustrated and upset because Mary isn't helping her with the work that she actually interrupts Jesus' teaching and asks Him to tell Mary to help her out.

Jesus responds to Martha by saying, *"You are so worried and bothered about so many things but only one thing is necessary. Martha was so troubled and distracted. Mary has chosen the good part and it won't be taken away from her."*

Mary had a focused heart, fixed on the Lord.

Nothing was wrong with Martha wanting to prepare the meal and serve her guests, but her heart wasn't in it. She was distracted.

What is your heart focusing on?

The Bible exhorts us, *"Let not your heart be troubled!"* Now, obviously, there are things in this life that have the potential to trouble us. However, Jesus exhorts us to *"Let not"* our hearts be troubled. This means *we* have the ability to choose to not be afraid, to not be anxious, and to not be worried.

Trust me, my experience tells me that is sometimes easier said than done!

Nine years ago, my husband Vinnie passed from this earthly life into his eternal reward of heaven. To say that was an easy experience for me to walk through couldn't be further from the truth.

Vinnie had battled in his physical body for years. Honestly, I believe he finally just got tired of fighting and so he went home to be with the Lord. While I was happy for him, knowing that his struggle was over, I was left a widow at 52 years of age. I was definitely way too young to be a widow!

In the years that followed, I experienced so many different emotions—disappointment, loneliness, frustration and depression. I've even questioned God and asked Him, "Why did this happen?" Honestly, I'm still not completely sure why my husband passed earlier than I would have ever expected, other than the fact that he was just tired of fighting.

I have come to accept that there are some things in this life that we just won't understand or be able to explain. We'll know all things when we get to heaven and then I don't think it will matter much.

What I have come to discover during this transition is the overwhelming love and faithfulness of my heavenly Father. I had only thought I knew what it meant to trust God before.

I have learned from this part of my journey that God alone is trustworthy. He's always good. He's always looking out for me and protecting me.

My heavenly Father is the one who has held me together all these years, and He won't ever let go of His hold on me. I am convinced of His love for me and believe my best days are just ahead of me.

God's word remains my constant source of strength and joy. Without it, I would not have made it through. If not for the many years of the "seed" of the

Word being sown into my heart, I wouldn't have overcome.

By the grace of God, I have overcome the grief and pain of losing my husband. Today I am strong and full of God's peace.

I am strong in the Lord and the power of His might. I have experienced the keeping and overcoming power of God's word.

His Word has never failed me and it never will. And, because He is no respecter of persons, His Word will never fail you either.

> *God Himself has said, I will not in any way fail you* nor *give you up* nor *leave you without support. I will not, I will not, I will not in any degree leave you helpless* nor *forsake* nor *let you down (relax My hold on you)! Assuredly not!*
> Hebrews 13:5 AMPC

Unbelief

We truly do have to choose daily to guard our hearts. One of the most crucial steps to take for our wellbeing is to protect our hearts from unbelief. Unbelief can come against us in many different ways.

Maybe you're experiencing a physical battle, for example. You are standing and declaring the Word of God. You are believing the report of the Lord. The next day you go the doctor for a check-up and he comes back with a report that sounds like bad news.

In that moment, you are faced with making a decision. While I'm not against doctors, we do have to be very careful with the words that we allow to be spoken over us.

> *We must at that point decide what thoughts we will allow to take up residence in our hearts.*

I used to believe that if I wasn't seeing an answer to prayer it must have been because I didn't have enough faith. I've come to know that isn't always the case. It is possible to have faith in God's word but to also have unbelief operating at the same time.

The unbelief is the real problem. Our unbelief can negate or water down the effectiveness of the Word of God that we are trying to believe.

How do you know if you truly believe?

Begin by asking yourself if you accept something as true or genuine? Do you have a firm or wholehearted conviction? Are you fully persuaded?

Our faith is belief in or a confident attitude towards God. This also involves commitment to His will for our life and placing one's trust in God's trust. A person who believes is one who takes God at His word.

Isn't that exactly what happens to us at salvation? We place our lives and trust in what Christ did on the cross. We believe in our hearts first, and then we confess with our mouths.

1. We must believe in our hearts that God's word is true.

2. We must believe that He loves us.

3. We must believe that He is always good and is worthy of our trust.

Right believing really is everything and is integral to our guarding our hearts. Truly, we must learn and put into practice how to keep guard and protect our hearts. It is part of our faith journey and it certainly requires diligence on our part.

You see, the condition of our heart will determine how we respond during pressure.

> *We can feed our fears by meditating on those fearful thoughts or we can grab a hold of them and say, "I will not allow fear to operate in my heart in Jesus name.*

Dr. Henry Cloud says, "You'll have what you tolerate." I believe that means that whatever we allow and put up with will not exit our lives.

I want to remind you that fear does not come from God. The Bible says—

God has not given us a spirit of fear but of
power, love and a sound mind.
2 Timothy 1:17 NKJV

Fear is a spirit and you must not give it any place.

One of my favorite scriptures is found in 1 John 4:18, *"There is no fear in love; but perfect love casts out all fear"* (NASB). When we truly get a revelation of just how much God loves us, then we have no reason to ever be fearful. Isn't that good news!

As I've already shared, 2 Corinthians 10:5 exhorts us to bring every thought captive to the Word of God. You must cast down any thoughts that are contrary to the Word.

Tear down unbelief, fear and anything
else that is in opposition to the truth.

The key is to immediately take hold of the negative thought or emotion. I am not saying it is always easy to do, but it is simple. Become vigilant and determined that nothing is allowed to steal your peace and joy.

Truly, what we feed will grow and what we starve will die. Feed your soul by sowing God's Word and you'll starve those peace stealers to death!

Focus!

The enemy knows that, *"The joy of the Lord is your strength"* (Nehemiah 8:10), and that's why he tries so hard to steal it from you.

Ask yourself, am I experiencing peace and joy? If not, chances are you are not guarding your heart and you are not keeping your thoughts focused on the right things.

Our circumstances won't stand a chance of moving us away from God's plan if we keep our hearts fixed upon Him. So where is your focus?

Have you ever thought about the word e-motion? It includes the word motion. Just as motion can mean to move up or down, so our emotions or feelings can move up and down too.

I'm reminded of the lyrics from an old song from the 1970's, "Feelings, nothing more than feelings". In other words, you can't trust your feelings because your feelings change all of time. Based upon the situation you find yourself, in whether good or bad, your mood can easily fluctuate.

Your feelings will try to move you in a certain direction. Our feelings can be caused by pain or pleasure, but they are only temporary. But, it's through our feelings that the enemy often tries to manipulate us. He tries to seduce us by using our feelings to move us away from the will of God.

That's why it is so vital that we don't give authority or permission to our feelings and emotions. We can't allow our feelings to get the best of us.

*I like to say that my feelings don't get a
vote. That means that anything I'm
feeling that is contrary to the Word of
God isn't allowed to move me.*

I don't mean to sound like I've gotten this discipline
mastered yet, but I choose to "work it" every day. I
don't always get it right, but I am determined to walk
by the Word and not by my feelings.

*If you can control your emotions, you
can do anything.*

I have emotions but my emotions will not have me!
Our emotions can harm and sidetrack our faith. We
must choose to not be ruled by our emotions and
feelings.

Jesus experienced emotions, but He never allowed
them to rule Him. As believers who want to grow up
in Christ we, too, must learn to master this area of our
lives and not be ruled by our feelings and our "sense"
realm.

As I choose to spend more time feeding upon the
Word of God and standing on the promises, I have
learned that my feelings will catch up.

What should you think about?

So what are your thinking on or what is your inner perspective or focus? Another of my favorite scriptures is found in the book of Philippians 4:6, 7—

> *Do not be anxious about anything, but in everything by prayer and supplication with thanksgiving let your requests be made known to God. And the peace of God that surpasses all understanding will guard your hearts and minds through Christ Jesus. (ESV)*

Most Biblical scholars agree that the apostle Paul wrote the book of Philippians while he was being held in prison. Paul found himself in a situation which was completely out of his control. Maybe you, too, find yourself in a place today that seems completely out of your control.

What is so amazing is that Paul had peace even in the midst of his very difficult and uncomfortable surroundings.

You see, we are going to miss out if we think peace is determined by what's going on in our natural lives. Our peace isn't based on outward circumstances but by what is found on the inside of us. It may seem like all hell is breaking loose around you but you can still experience peace.

*The truth is that real peace is only
found through Jesus Christ himself.*

Charles Spurgeon defined God's peace as, "The unruffled serenity of the infinitely happy God, the eternal composure of the absolutely well-contented God."

God's peace transcends our ability to understand with the natural mind. It just doesn't always make sense.

We have all experienced His supernatural peace deep on the inside when things around us certainly wouldn't call for peace.

God's peace will guard your heart and mind. The word guard in this scripture speaks of a military action. That's what God's peace does for us.

*His peace is on guard over our hearts
and minds.*

I previously shared Colossians 3:1, 2: *"Therefore if you have been raised up with Christ, keep seeking the things above, where Christ is, seated at the right hand of God. Set your mind on things above, not on things that are on the earth"* (NASB).

This means we must choose to set our hearts and minds on God's truths, and keep them fixed. Don't be moved off the mark! This passage is literally saying that we are to seek after the eternal, to seek after God's kingdom. We can choose to set our hearts, our minds and our affections on the higher things, on God's priorities. Seek Him, inquire of Him and meditate on Him. We set our heart and mind on Him when we think about how good He is and how much He loves us.

Colossians 3:15 reminds us to, *"Let the peace of Christ rule in your hearts."* I really like how the Passion Translation reads, *"Let your hearts always be guided by the peace of the Anointed One."*

I've come to the place in my life that I desire living in peace and joy more than anything else. I hope you'll make that decision for yourself too. Will you feed your fears and anxieties by listening to negative people and negative reports? Will you allow negative thoughts that are contrary to the Word steal from you? Will you continue to be moved by what you see and what you feel or, will you choose to be moved by what God has said? My prayer is that you will choose the latter!

5
WATCH YOUR MOUTH

MANY BOOKS HAVE BEEN WRITTEN ABOUT the power of our words. I have often wondered, "Then why do we seem to struggle so much in this area?"

I'm sure we can all agree that the words we speak are extremely important. The Bible makes it clear that, *"Death and life is in the power of the tongue and those who love it will eat its fruit"* (Proverbs 18:21 NASB).

So ask yourself the question, am I speaking life or am I speaking death? Do I really take the words I speak seriously?

If we are being honest, we would probably have to admit that we don't take them seriously enough. Perhaps we don't place enough value upon the words we speak.

The Holy Spirit continues to speak to me about the importance of this truth: *"A good man out of the good treasure of his heart brings forth good; and an evil man out of the evil treasure of his heart brings forth evil. For*

out of the abundance of the heart the mouth speaks."
Luke 6:45 (NKJV).

> *You don't have to be around someone*
> *for very long to know what's in their*
> *heart because their words give it away.*

The words we speak depend upon what's filling up our hearts. What is filling up your heart today? Anxiety? Fear? Depression? Discouragement? Or, peace and joy?

Words are Creative and Powerful

> *By faith we understand the worlds were*
> *prepared by the Word of God so that what is*
> *seen was not made out of the things which*
> *are visible.*
> Hebrews 11:3 NASB

This is so powerful. God literally spoke our physical world into existence by His words.

Do you know that your words also have creative power? The word of God is alive and it is powerful. When we speak His words our situations have to change.

The apostle James wrote about the power of our smallest member, the tongue. James calls the tongue a fire that can defile our entire body. Our words can set the direction for our day and the course for our lives. Your words can also derail the direction of your life.

We can use our words to build up or to tear down. We should be slow to speak and not just run off at the mouth. That's especially challenging for those of us that enjoy talking so much.

James goes on to say that if we are able to control our words, we will be able to control ourselves in every way. That is ● what James calls "real maturity."

We must teach ourselves to speak by faith by lining up our words with the Word of God. We must begin speaking faith-filled words and not words that are based on our feelings. You can speak life over any situation or circumstance.

God's Word is God's will for you. I'm going to say that again.

God's Word is God's will for you!

Nourish Yourself with the Word of God

Matthew 12:34 says, *"Out of the abundance of the heart the mouth speaks"* (NKJV). This means whatever you are feeding on and sowing into your thought life will come out of your mouth.

We don't automatically think and speak the way God does. We must make a decision to feed on God's word and then our thinking will change.

Our way of speaking will also change. There is always a direct correlation between our words and what we are daily feeding ourselves.

What we spend the most time thinking about is what you will believe and will in turn speak about.

Matthew 12:35 continues by saying, *The good man* BRINGS *out of his good treasure what is good; and the evil man brings out of his evil treasure what is evil"* (NASB).

This paints such a vivid picture of the power of our words doesn't it? The good treasure referred to in this passage is speaking of our heart.

The correlation that is being made between a good man and an evil man is by the words that they are speaking.

If we're sowing God's word into our heart, then His words will be what we speak. Literally, what you put in is what will come out.

We can be snared by the words of our mouths.

If you're a person that is prone to saying everything that comes into your mind, you're going to really need to get a handle on this truth.

I want to ask you today to consider if you need to change what you've been speaking?

Maybe you have a situation in your life that needs to change. What are you saying about it? Or better yet what are you saying to it?

Do you spend more time talking about the situation as it currently is, or are you speaking and declaring what the Word of God says about it?

Jesus' Powerful Words

Consider this account in Mark 11:11-24. The passage begins with Jesus cursing a fig tree. He was hungry and saw a fig tree in the distance. Obviously, He was hoping to enjoy a figgy snack, but He soon realized that there was not one fig to be found on the tree.

In Israel, this type of fig tree would produce fruit even before the leaves had appeared.

Jesus then cursed the tree, "May no one ever eat fruit from you again!"

Can you imagine being there and hearing Jesus talking to that tree?

Notice it says that "His disciples were listening". They were right there next to Him, listening. The truth is they didn't believe or understand what was really happening.

The next morning Jesus and the disciples passed by the same fig tree. The disciples were shocked to see

ROBIN CIOFFI

that the tree had withered from the roots up. Peter spoke up—

> *Rabbi, look, the fig tree which You cursed has*
> *withered.*
> *V. 21 NASB*

I guess Peter had not really expected that the words Jesus had spoken would accomplish what He had said. The scripture says Jesus answered Peter and said, "Have faith in God. (v. 22)

We could also say it this way: "Let the faith of God be in you." This means that we literally have God's faith.

It's not about you using just your own
faith. It's knowing that God's faith is
working in and through you.

That is a powerful truth that we need to get in our hearts.

Speak to Your Mountain

The account in Mark continues with Jesus teaching His disciples the importance of "speaking to the mountain".

A mountain is anything in your life that is a hindrance or an obstacle that needs to be removed.

Oftentimes we speak to God about the mountain rather than speaking to the mountain for ourselves.

84

We must begin using our God-given authority and speak to the mountains that are standing against us. We need to say what God says.

Please get hold of this truth. It isn't enough to just have faith but your faith must be spoken with authority.

Faith is released through our words when we speak God's Words.

> *God's power can be voice-activated.*
> *Speak His Word and His power will*
> *show up on your behalf.*

We read another example of this truth in Mark 4:39, 40.

The disciples were out on the sea while Jesus is sleeping in the stern of the boat. The winds and waves were so strong that the boat was filling up with water.

The disciples were afraid and especially troubled because Jesus was sound asleep. Finally, they couldn't take it any longer and they woke up Jesus.

I'm sure Jesus would have been pretty ticked with them for disturbing His sleep, but He got up. Then He rebuked the wind and the waves, *"Hush! Be still!"* (v. 39 NASB).

Immediately the wind died down and the sea calmed.

Please notice that Jesus didn't pray about the storm—He spoke to it.

Faith Declarations

This is such a powerful truth to get in our spirits and to put into practice for ourselves. As believers we often spend time praying about a situation while we could have been speaking to the situation instead. We need to command our situations to change according to the Word of God, and believe that they will change!

I suggest that right now you write down anything going on in your life that isn't God's will for you.

Are you depressed? Are you battling sickness? Do you need a job? Is your marriage falling apart? Whatever the situation is, write it down.

Next, find scriptures that you can speak over your personal situation. These scriptures will become your "Faith Declarations."

Here is an example: If you are experiencing health issues or battling sickness in your body, then make a list of healing scriptures.

- Declare that by the stripes of Jesus you are healed.
- Declare that with long life God will satisfy you and show you His salvation.
- There are so many scriptures that that tell us it's God's will for us to walk in health.

Start your day by making your faith declarations, speaking the scriptures out loud. You may also want to write down the scriptures on sticky notes and tape them on your refrigerator or bathroom mirror. This will really help you keep the Word coming out of your mouth.

Speak out your faith with the Word of God.

You will need to be consistent and intentional. No letting up. Allow the Word of God to change your reality. We must believe that the words we are speaking will come to pass.

We must always remember that God is not holding out on us. On the cross Jesus said, *"It is finished."*

God knew everything ahead of time that we would ever be faced with in this life, and He has already made provision for us to meet the need. We cannot allow any room for doubt or unbelief. Don't give them any place in your heart. Keep believing and receiving.

God's Word is the absolute authority and we must be committed to His truth.

Once you are fully persuaded, there will be no talking you out of it. You will pray His Word with authority. You will speak His Word with authority and you will have what you have declared in faith.

God's plan will manifest to the degree that we yield and speak His words from our hearts.

God's Word is the truth and it never changes. His Word is His promise to us, and it will not fail you.

For those of us who will plant His word in our hearts, we will see what we believe and what we speak to manifest.

I declare with you today that those mountains are moving right now out of your way in Jesus name.

FAITH DECLARATIONS

Here are some powerful declarations for you to speak. They represent who you are in Christ.

I am a child of God. John 1:12
I am a friend of God. John 15:15
I have been bought with a price. I Corinthians 6:19, 20
I am a new creation. 2 Corinthians 5:14-17
I have been redeemed and forgiven. Colossians 1:14
I am complete in Christ. Colossians 2:9, 10
I am loved by God. John 3:16, 17
I am healed by Jesus' stripes. I Peter 2:24
I am healed. Psalm 103:3
I am enjoying good health. 3 John 3
I am healed. Psalm 107:20
I am healed by His stripes. Isaiah 53:5
I have abundant life. John 10:10
I am free from condemnation. Romans 8:1, 2
I cannot be separated from the love of God. Romans 8:35
I am not fearful. 2 Timothy 1:7
I am hidden in Christ. Colossians 3:3
I am born of God and the evil one cannot touch me. IJohn 5:18
I am salt and light. Matthew 5:13, 14

I have been chosen and appointed to bear fruit. John 15:16

I am God's temple. I Corinthians 3:16

I am seated with Christ. Ephesians 2:6

I am God's workmanship. Ephesians 2:10

I am created by God. Psalm 139:13, 14

I am set free. John 8:31-32

I can do all things through Christ. Philippians 4:13

6
THINK YOURSELF HAPPY

THE LONGER I WALK WITH GOD THE MORE I have come to realize that I need to be able to encourage myself in the Lord.

I'm sure we all have that friend that we can call upon to cheer us up when we're feeling down. You know, that friend that just seems to always know exactly what to say to turn our bad mood right around.

Don't get me wrong, those kinds of friends are a blessing to our lives. But what happens when they're not around? Are you just going to spend the whole day feeling sad, depressed or discouraged?

I hope you'll take my advice and learn to encourage yourself in the Lord.

A How-to Lesson on Encouraging Yourself

You might think that sounds really good but wonder how to do that. Let me share a few practical ways to help you get started.

First, you need to learn how to glorify the Lord. What does it mean to glorify? By definition, the word *glorify* means to praise and worship God. We glorify Him when we honor Him and lift up His name. We glorify Him when we hold Him in high esteem.

He is worthy to be glorified because He is to be valued above everything and everyone else.

We glorify Him through our personal relationship with Him. Simply spending time talking to Him and thanking Him for all He's done for you is glorifying Him.

We glorify Him when we acknowledge how great He is. We glorify Him because He never changes. He is the same yesterday, today and forever. He is forever good. Forever faithful. Forever present and forever with us. Forever for us. There is truly no one like our God.

Another way I encourage myself in the Lord is by being thankful. Being thankful doesn't just happen automatically. We must choose to be intentional.

How about reminding yourself of how very deeply loved you are by God. God really is madly in love with you and nothing will ever change that truth.

I love how the Passion Translation reads in Psalms 139:17, 18—

Every single moment you are always thinking about me! How precious and wonderful to consider that you cherish me constantly in your every thought!

Now how about that for an encouraging word!

What about reminding yourself of all He has done for you? Are you saved today? Thank the Lord. Are you safe? Are you healthy? Have you ever experienced God's healing power?

Did you eat today? Do you have a roof over your head? Have you ever received answers to your prayers?

The list goes on and on but I think you're getting the idea. It's so good for us to remind ourselves of how blessed we really are.

I have found it really is impossible to stay down or defeated when you start reflecting on all your many blessings.

The 23rd Psalm is one of my favorites and ministers to me every time I read it. While many of us may have even memorized these verses, it's certainly worth our time to take a closer look at the words written by David.

Psalm 23:1-3 (NAS) reads, *"The Lord is my shepherd, I shall not want. He makes me lie down in green pastures; He restores my soul; He guides me in the path of righteousness for His name's sake."*

This passage paints such a beautiful picture for us. The word for "shepherd" here is taken from the root word *ra'ah* which is the Hebrew word for "best friend."

The Lord is our shepherd and our very best friend. He surely gives us everything we need.

I've had the great joy of visiting the land of Israel many times. On several occasions we would see shepherds in the fields watching over their sheep. At night, the shepherds lay outside the entrance of the sheep pen to guard and protect their flocks. The sheep are kept safe and are given everything they need.

This beautiful illustration is also true for us. Jesus is our shepherd. The picture of lying down in green pastures is a place of rest and peace for us, undisturbed from the enemy of our soul.

We can rest secure when we know that we have the good Shepherd watching over us.

I have found another powerful way to encourage myself—simply to magnify the Lord.

While that sounds so simple to do, it can really be challenging—especially at times when it seems that all hell is breaking out around you.

Magnify the Lord

A familiar story, found in the Book of Numbers, Chapters 13 and 14, provides a great example of magnifying the Lord. This is the story of the twelve spies. Moses sent them forth to spy out the Promised Land.

The spies had been gone for 40 days and had experienced many amazing things. They had seen the beautiful Promised Land overflowing with abundance. It was truly a land of milk and honey.

Of course, in addition to those amazing things there were also mighty giants dwelling in the land.

This story has such a powerful lesson for us to learn and to put into practice. All twelve spies saw the same Promised Land. But only two, Joshua and Caleb, came back with a victorious report. Isn't it interesting that Joshua and Caleb are the only two spies whose names were given in this biblical account?

The other ten spies focused on the giants in the land. The giants were so fearsome that the spies actually said, *"We became like grasshoppers in our own sight, and so we were in their sight"* (Numbers 13:33 NASB).

The ten spies had totally forgotten all the miracles that God had done for them. They had seen God part the Red Sea and the Egyptian armies defeated. God had provided for them through the wilderness. Sadly, they chose to focus on the giants instead.

Joshua and Caleb had seen the very same giants, but they said, *"Let us go up at once and take possession, for we are well able to overcome it"* (v. 30 NKJV).

Joshua and Caleb were determined and convinced of God's promises. God told them that He was going to give them that land and they believed Him. They also chose to focus on what God had done for them in the past and they were strong in their faith.

**They chose to focus on His promises
and they magnified Him.**

They knew the giants were there, but they chose not to focus on them. They kept their focus on the Lord.

This is so simple but so very profound. It really hits us between the eyes. God has already done so much for us, His children. Why is it that it seems to be so hard to believe Him when we're facing our own giants?

Can I suggest that maybe it's because we are choosing to magnify the problems more than the

Problem Solver? Maybe we're focusing on the giants rather than the promises of the Promise Keeper.

Our problems always try to speak to us and then they will be magnified in our eyes. We are faced with a dilemma that requires us to make a decision.

Shut Up, Giant!

We can be like those ten spies and forget the promises of God. We can focus on the giants just like they did. Or, we can be like Joshua and Caleb. They saw the giants, but they chose to not be moved by them. They reminded themselves of the promises of God and remembered all He had done for them.

They magnified the Lord instead of magnifying the giants.

That's exactly what we need to do when the giants seem to be standing in our way. If we allow the giants to speak to us we will cower in fear.

Fear is a powerful weapon that the enemy will try to use against you.

Fear will open the door to the enemy and give him a place to operate. We must not allow him any room. Don't crack the door open even a little for him.

Have you ever seen the acrostic for the word FEAR? "False Evidence Appearing Real." That's the thing about fear. It isn't really real, but it rises from our emotions or from our soul realm.

Fear is based upon the "what ifs" of life and not on the truth. It usually concerns something that will never even happen. It's based on what we can see or feel with our physical senses and not based upon the Word of God.

The Bible speaks about fear as having torment but His *"perfect love casts out all fear."* (I John 4:18 NKJV). When we allow a spirit of fear to operate, we certainly aren't going to be experiencing God's peace and joy.

Remember that the Bible calls fear a "spirit." A spirit of fear will rob you of your peace and your sense of wellbeing. That is always the work of the enemy. Jesus said, *"The thief does not come except to steal, and to kill and to destroy. I have come that they might have life and that they may have it more abundantly"* John 10:10 (NKJV).

We all know that in this life no one is exempt from troubles and challenges. However, we have the ability to choose what we will focus on and what we will believe.

God, help us to be like Joshua and Caleb. Let us be so totally convinced of God's promises so that we will go up and possess all that He has provided for us.

Blessed to be a Blessing

I have found another powerful way to encourage myself. That is by simply reaching out to be a blessing to someone. It may be sharing a kind word or just a smile. It can be as simple as giving an encouraging word or a hug to someone who is having a hard day. Or maybe, it's making a phone call or just sending a text.

I have found that by taking my eyes off of me and looking to bless someone else, I end up feeling so much better. Ephesians 6:8 says that *"whatever good anyone does, he will receive the same from the Lord"* (NKJV).

Shift the focus from yourself and look for opportunities to make a difference. It's amazing that what often seems so small or insignificant can make a big impact in someone's life.

Hope

This brings me to one of my favorite subjects: *hope*. What is hope? The biblical definition for hope is the confident expectation of what God has promised. I'd say that's the confident expectation of something good!

Hope looks forward to something with desire and speaks of the future. Hope believes that God has done what He said He would do.

There are several words in Hebrew for hope. One is *chacah* and means to flee for protection, to trust, to have hope or to make a refuge.

Another word is *mibtach* and it means confidence, trust, hope and assurance.

The hope I'm speaking of here isn't the same as saying, "I hope this will work out," or "I hope this will happen."

> **The hope I'm referring to is the**
> **confident expectation that what God**
> **has promised will surely come to pass.**

Martin Luther said, "Faith looks to the promises of God's Word. Hope looks to the good and the benefits that come from His promises."

Our hope in the Lord brings us security and confidence. Hope is extremely powerful and always brings us encouragement.

We read in Romans 15:13, *"May the God of hope fill you with all joy and peace as you trust in Him, so that you may overflow with hope by the power of the Holy Spirit"* (NIV)

Having hope focuses our attention on God and fills us with expectation until we see the manifestation in the natural realm.

Jeremiah 29:11 encourages us, *"For I know the plans I have for you declares the Lord, plans for good and not for harm; plans to give you a hope and a future"* (NIV).

The truth is God has never failed us yet and He never will. As long as our trust is in the Lord, we will have hope and a future.

Praying in the Spirit

Praying in the Spirit (praying in tongues) is a great way to encourage yourself. If you have not yet experienced the precious baptism or infilling of the Holy Spirit, then you are missing out on a precious gift and blessing.

The infilling of the Holy Spirit is not just for a select few. The infilling of the Holy Spirit is for every born-again believer.

Acts Chapter 2 records the account of the Holy Spirit coming upon the disciples in the upper room on the day of Pentecost.

When the Holy Spirit came upon the disciples, *"they were all filled with the Holy Spirit and began to speak with other tongues as the Spirit gave them utterance"* (Acts 2:4 NKJV).

If you have received Jesus as your Lord, then you can receive this precious gift of the Holy Spirit. You just need to ask and receive by faith.

*Ask, and it will be given to you; seek, and you
will find; knock, and it will be opened to you.
For everyone who asks receives, and he who
seeks finds, and to him who knocks it will be
opened. Or what man is there among you
who, if his son asks for bread, will give him a
stone? Or if he asks for a fish, will he give him
a serpent? If you then, being evil, know how to
give good gifts to your children, how much
more will your Father who is in heaven give
good things to those who ask Him!*
Matthew 7:7-11 NKJV

Your heavenly Father is the very best father and He wants to give you this precious gift of the Holy Spirit. Simply ask Him and he will fill you to overflowing. Truly your life will never be the same!

1 Corinthians 14:4 instructs us that, *"The one who speaks in tongues edifies himself"* (NASB). You can literally build yourself up by praying in tongues.

Are you feeling down or depressed today? If so, I encourage you to practice praying in the Spirit. You will be refreshed and restored.

Jude, verse 20, tells us, *"But you, beloved, building yourselves up on your most holy faith, praying in the Holy Spirit."* (NASB). Praying in the Spirit is powerful and it's supernatural.

When we pray in tongues, we bypass our human minds and our spirit prays. When we pray in the Spirit we are speaking directly to God. The Holy Spirit is praying through us. It is supernatural, edifies us and builds us up, and is so very powerful..

Our enemy, the devil, isn't able to understand what we're saying when we pray in tongues. The communication is straight from the Holy Spirit to the Father.

The Holy Spirit will often speak to you as you're praying and reveal hidden things to you. You can pray in tongues when you just don't know what to pray in English or whatever your native tongue is. The apostle Paul expanded on this in Romans 8:26 (NASB)—

In the same way the Spirit helps our weaknesses; for we don't always know how to pray as we should, but the Spirit Himself intercedes for us with groanings too deep for words.

The Greek word for *helps* in this scripture means "the Spirit lays hold together against the enemy." Praying in the Spirit is an effective spiritual weapon that we can use every day.

Holy Spirit is always with you

I want to encourage you to remember that the Holy Spirit is with you always. If you're born again, then He is on the inside of you and walks beside you. He is your helper and your comforter. The enemy will try to make you feel all alone but he's just a liar. Pay him no mind.

The truth is that you're never alone. We just need to be more mindful of the Holy Spirit's presence in our lives. I want to encourage you to be more conscious and intentional in reminding yourself of this truth. Go ahead and call upon Him. He is always there with you and for you.

I have found another great way to encourage myself is by calling to remembrance God's faithfulness.

You can begin by reminding yourself of all the times He's answered your cries for help.

How about reminding yourself of all the times He's answered your prayers. What about all the times He made a way when you just didn't see how things would work out.

It is so amazing what happens to us when we start thinking about just how good our God is. That reminds me of one of my favorite scriptures found in the book of Psalms—

*I would have fainted if I had not believed to
see the goodness of the Lord in the land of the
living.*
Psalms 27:13 KJV

The New Living Translation reads, *"I am confident
I will see the Lord's goodness while I'm here in the land of
the living."*

Ask yourself this question: Am I confident in the
Lord's goodness? I imagine you will be able to answer
that question with an overwhelmingly confident Yes!

The real key is that we must choose to remind
ourselves of His goodness. Call to mind our victories
of the past.

Heaven is in Our Future!

In closing, another way I encourage myself in the
Lord is to think about the future. I'm referring to our
eternal future with the Lord—the heavenly home that
awaits us as believers in Christ.

Oftentimes we get so caught up with what is going
on right now in our natural lives that we forget that this
is all just temporary. We are simply passing through this
temporal life.

While God certainly wants us to enjoy our lives in
the "here and now," at its best our earthly life is nothing
in comparison with the glorious life that is ahead of us.

One day Jesus will split through the skies and take His bride out of this old world.

I find it disturbing that we don't hear much teaching about heaven unless we're attending a memorial service. Then we are reminded of how glorious heaven will be.

As a young Christian, I used to hear the statement that someone was "so heavenly minded that they were of no earthly good." People would throw that phrase around because those saints were so focused on the return of Christ and going to heaven.

When was the last time you were with someone who was just too heavenly minded? I surely can't remember such a time.

While being too caught up with heaven may hinder us being as fruitful and productive as we could be, I'm afraid we've swung too far toward the other side of the spectrum.

I get excited and am encouraged when I think about the return of the Lord. I really can't help but smile. Just think about it for a moment. No more of this world's mess and all its flaws. No more sin, no more pain, no more sickness, no more sadness, no more loss and no more suffering of any kind.

Folks, heaven is going to be beyond amazing! We will finally see Jesus face to face. We will see our loved ones that have gone on before us.

We will also get a new heavenly body. Might I add it will be a perfect body.

Not only that but we will be returning to a new heaven and a new earth. We will all be together with the Lord and all His saints forever.

We can boldly say, "Even so, come quickly, Lord Jesus."

In the meantime, remember that God truly wants you to live a full life and experience His abundance in the here and now—not only because He loves you, but because He loves the whole world.

While there is still time, let us keep on pressing forward to what lies ahead. Keep fighting the good fight of faith. Look to Jesus, the Author and the Finisher of your faith.

Beloved, run the race set before you! May we all live lives worthy of the calling of Christ until that glorious day when we hear, *"Well done, thou good and faithful servant."*

Made in the USA
Monee, IL
27 July 2020

37096472R00066